# mybook

## just for ME

SO DON'T EVEN THINK
ABOUT OPENING IT!

D0068460

SCHOLASTIC INC.

ISBN 978-0-545-48497-8

12 11 10 9 8 7 6 5 4 3 2 1          13 14 15 16 17 18/0

Printed in China          84

First printing, January 2013

Written by *Gabby Brooks*
Art Direction by *Paul W. Banks*
Designed by *Rocco Melillo*
Spot Illustrations by *Deena Fleming*

# ABOUT THIS BOOK:

THIS BOOK IS ABOUT WHO U ARE! IT'S PACKED FULL OF QUIZZES, ACTIVITIES, AND TONS OF OTHER STUFF, SO WHAT ARE U WAITING FOR? TURN THE PAGE AND GET STARTED!

SECTION 1:
mystatus

SECTION 2:
myswag

SECTION 3:
mybesties

SECTION 4:
myplaylist

SECTION 5:
myschool

SECTION 6:
MYFUTURE

# THIS
# BOOK
# IS
# MY BOOK

Kayla

your name here

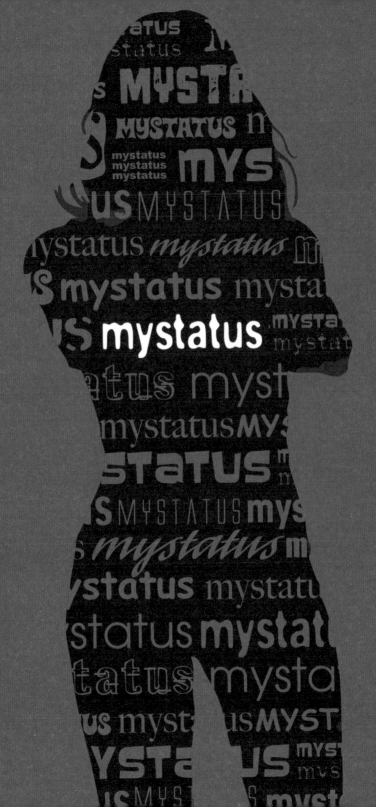

# MY DEETS
↰ (details)

75: What's ur name? _Kayla_ 74: When is ur birthday?
_Dec 26_ 73: If u could describe yourself in
one word, what would it be?_____ 72: Who's ur
bestie? _Rachel_ 71: Longest friendship? _my life_
70: Are u single? _no_ 69: Who's ur crush? _?_
_____ 68: How old are u? _9_ 67: What color are
ur eyes? _brown_ 66: Glasses or contacts? 65: What
color is ur hair? _brown_ 64: How many siblings do u
have? _?_ 63: Do u have a pet? _no_ 62: What's its name/
what would its name be if u had one?_____
61: How tall are u?_____ 60: What state do u live
in? _NJ_ 59: If u could live in another state, which
one would it be? _?_____

## FAVS-
58: What's ur favorite word?
_Ipad_
57: Musician?_____
56: Actress?_____
55: Actor?_____
54: Animal? _puppy_
53: Book for school?
_____
52: Book for fun? _Diary
of a wimpy kid_
51: Movie? _The_
50: TV show? _Wizards_

49: Food? _Sushi_
48: Color? _purple_
47: Ice cream? _cake batter_
46: Veggie?_____
45: Fruit?_____
44: Relative?_____
43: Lip gloss flavor?_____
42: Makeup brand?_____
41: Superhero? _mom\dad_
40: What's ur fav thing
about yourself?_____
_____

# HIDDEN TALENTS-

39: Can u do a split? NO  38: Play an instrument? YES

37: Do u speak another language? YES (pig Latin counts)

36: What game are u the best at? _____

35: One thing u wish u knew how to do? _____

# CIRCLE 1 OF 3-

34: texter/talker/tweeter?  33: shy/social/super-friendly?

32: (tv)/music/books?  31: (milk shake/sundae/cupcake?)

30: sweet/salty/(sour)?  29: drama/comedy/romance?

28: breakfast/lunch/(dinner)?  27: buttons/zippers/(snaps)?

26: (swimming)/tanning/lifeguard-spotting?

25: spearmint/cinnamon/fruity?  24: plane/boat/train?

23: (pancakes/waffles/French toast?)

# LOGGED ON-

22: When r u not online? _____  21: Funniest You-
Tube video? _____  20: Most-played app? _____

# INSIDE INFO-

19: What color is ur underwear today? _____

18: Where are u most ticklish? _____  17: What do u
notice 1st in a guy? _____  16: Last time u
laughed? _____  15: Last time u cried? _____

14: Friend u r jealous of? _____  13: Last song u
listened to? _____  12. Last song u sang? _____

11: Where do u do ur homework? _____  10: Ever pulled
an all-nighter? ___  9: Best b-day ever? _____

# TBH-

8: Last told a lie? _____  7: Does love
at first sight exist? ___  6: Best EVER fortune from a
fortune cookie? _____  5: Good luck charm?
_____  4: Any phobias? ___  3: Do u like roller
coasters? ___  2: Nickname? _____

1: Did u tell the truth when answering these questions? ___

# ABC's of Me

Actress u most look like: _____

BFFs: Joey   Julian   lindsay  Rachel
Summy  Jade

Can't live without: ___Julian \ Rache
family

Desserts are_____.

English or math?  math_____

Friend u last chilled with:_____

Gift u last received:_____

Habits (good or bad!): ___good_____

If I could be anything, I'd be_____.

Jock or not?_____

Key to ur heart:_____

Last text message was from:  Rachel

Memory u'd like to erase:_____

Never did I ever_____.

Oops! I shouldn't have_____.

Person u can count on:_____

Quick pick — puppy or kitty?_____

Relationships are_____.

Shampoo scent:_____

Top pet peeve: _____

UFOs are_____.

Video game that's ur fav:_____

Who do u love?_____

Xactly who is ur secret crush?_____

Y do u like this book so much?_____

Zzzz . . . when did u fall asleep last night?_____

m
n
o
p
q
r
s
t
u
v
w
x
y
z

# family tree

Label family members, friends, pets,
and anyone close to u in ur family tree.
After all, ur friends ARE ur family!
Feel free to paste in photos, too!

# WOULD U RATHER...

(circle answer)

Attend a concert or a dance party?

Receive chocolates or flowers?

Travel to the beach or the big city?

Eat an ice-cream cone or a snow cone?

Write with a pencil or a pen?

Eat cupcakes or cake pops?

Wear ur hair in a ponytail or a bun?

Read a magazine article or a book?

Stay warm with a scarf or earmuffs?

Listen to one song or the entire album?

Drink a soda or a smoothie?

Have fun roller-skating or ice-skating?

Make extra money by being a babysitter or a camp counselor?

Rock a turtleneck or a V-neck?

Use a laptop or a desktop?

Take a bath or a shower?

# UR LIFE IS AMAZING!

Draw a movie poster that
would make the story of ur life a blowout at the box office!

# Crushing Hard . . . OR HARDLY CRUSHING?

List ur Top 5 non-negotiables for a crush:

1. _____
2. _____
3. _____
4. _____
5. _____

## If u had to choose when it comes to ur crush . . .

blue eyes   or   brown eyes?

musician   or   math wiz?

dark hair   or   light hair?

jock   or   brainiac?

taller   or   shorter?

shy guy   or   life of the party?

straight hair   or   curly hair?

## List ur #1 celeb crush in each category:

☐ Pro athlete _____

☐ Movie star _____

☐ Musician _____

☐ TV star _____

☐ Reality star _____

*If ur crush could be most like any of these celebs, who would u pick?*

# What Kind of Texter R U?

**How long does it take u to respond to a txt?**

- A. 5 seconds
- B. 1–2 minutes
- C. did I even get a txt msg?

**If u misspell something, u . . .**

- A. let it slide.
- B. fix it before u send it.
- C. fix it only if it's sooo wrong ur meaning would be lost.

**How lengthy r ur txts?**

- A. few paragraphs
- B. few sentences
- C. few words

**Which are u most likely to txt?**

- A. c u 2nite
- B. see u tonite
- C. see u tonight

**If someone responds to ur txt with "K," u . . .**

- A. get upset—they're totally blowing u off!
- B. think maybe they're busy.
- C. think, "It's all the same to me!"

# RESULTS

## MOSTLY A's:

*U r a
Text-a-holic!*

Texting = ur life.
Texting is an
art and u r
Michelangelo.

## MOSTLY B's:

*U r a
Typical Texter:*

Texting is
an important
part of ur life, but
not essential.
U check ur
phone every
now and then.

## MOSTLY C's:

*U r a
Rare Texter:*

Texting isn't all
that important
to u. U prefer
convos in person
or on the phone.
Tone of voice is
everything.

# Text Fails

Whether it's an auto-correction nightmare or a text sent to the wrong person, this happens to everyone! Write ur biggest text fails here.

# EAT UP

## Yuck!
What's the nastiest food you've had?

## IDK...
If u were a food, what would u be?

## S.O.S.!
If u could eat only one food, what would it be?

## Yum!
What is ur fav dessert?

## I'm craving...
Chocolaty or fruity snacks?

## Top Chef
What's the best food you've whipped up in the kitchen?

## Check, Please!
Do u dine in or take out?

## Partay!
At ur b-day din, what is ur perf meal?

# PEAKS & PITS

EVERYONE HAS THEIR PITS (BAD TIMES) AND PEAKS (GOOD TIMES). FILL IN UR
GOOD TIMES ON THE PEAKS OF THESE MOUNTAINS . . . U KNOW WHERE TO PUT UR PITS!

PEAK

PEAK

PEAK

PEAK

PIT

PIT

# ONLINE 101

## Fill in the blanks:

I hide _____ on my web/blog page.

I _____ accept friend requests.

I change my password _____.

I'm always on www. _____.

My relationship status is _____.

If something fun happens to me it takes me _____ minutes to post it.

I check my email _____ times a day.

I have _____ friends.

I have _____ websites bookmarked.

I update my status _____.

Blogs are _____.

Fav PIC here:

*My Top 3 websites:*

1. _____

2. _____

3. _____

# What's Ur Fashion Persona?

## TOTALLY!

The one piece of clothing I can't live without is my . . .

A. leopard-print coat.
B. breezy mesh shorts.
C. cozy knit sweater.

## CA-CHING!

If I had a gift card for my fav clothing store, I'd spend it on a . . .

A. one-of-a-kind jacket.
B. fitted jeans without rips.
C. floral dress.

## STRUT IT!

My fav shoes are . . .

A. glam high heels.
B. colorful flip-flops.
C. strappy flat sandals.

## ALL MINE!

My policy on sharing clothes is . . .

A. I don't share.
B. only if we're besties.
C. I share my clothes all the time.

## BLING!

My fav accessories are . . .

A. glitzy jewelry.
B. sleek watches.
C. aviator sunglasses.

## BOTTOMS UP!

At the beach, I usually wear a . . .

A. bikini with a hot pattern.
B. single-color one-piece.
C. floral bikini with a floppy hat.

# RESULTS

## MOSTLY A's:

*U r a Fashionista.*

U make bold choices and set trends!

## MOSTLY B's:

*U r a Prepster.*

U keep it comfy b/c u r always on the go!

## MOSTLY C's:

*U r a Bohemian.*

U have a free spirit and a laid-back casual style!

# TOP 5 MUST-HAVES

Everyone has pieces of clothing they simply MUST HAVE. Cut out ur Top 5 Must-Haves from different magazines and paste them below . . . *in order of preference!*

# RED CARPET
## MOMENTS

**T**he red carpet is where fashion statements are made (and fashion disasters explode!). List ur fav red-carpet fashion moments below! If u have mag clips to add, even better!

# How Do U ACCESSORIZE?

**My accessories are...**

- A. simple.
- B. a statement.

**I make sure my accessories...**

- A. match, match, match.
- B. stand out.

**When it comes to my BLING, I always choose...**

- A. delicate necklaces.
- B. chunky bangles.

**At school, I...**

- A. wear the same accessory most of the time.
- B. always switch up my accessories.

**In a skirt or dress, I prefer...**

- A. solid leggings.
- B. patterned tights.

**My perf purse fits...**

- A. just enough.
- B. everything.

# RESULTS

## MOSTLY A's

**Simply Chic.**

U keep it simple. U don't want ur accessories to steal UR show.

## MOSTLY B's

**Fashionista.**

Ur accessories make ur outfit. Plain clothes are just not enough for u!

# GET DRESSED!

## What would u wear with... (circle answer)

**Maxi dress:**
standout belt or statement necklace?

**Patterned shorts:**
chunky wedges or ballet flats?

**Bold-colored blazer:**
white tank or clashing shirt?

**Black romper:**
neon sandals or dangly earrings?

**Leggings:**
tight tunic or flowy shirt?

# Prom

The prom outfits below could use some stylish add-ons. Make ur mark by adding frills, jewelry, or anything else u think would complete their looks. U could even cut out fav fashion finds from magazines and glue them here!

# morP

Take ur style intuition to the next
level by designing morp outfits, head to toe!
Design any outfit u wish, any way u wish . . .
After all, these fab looks are for the backward prom!

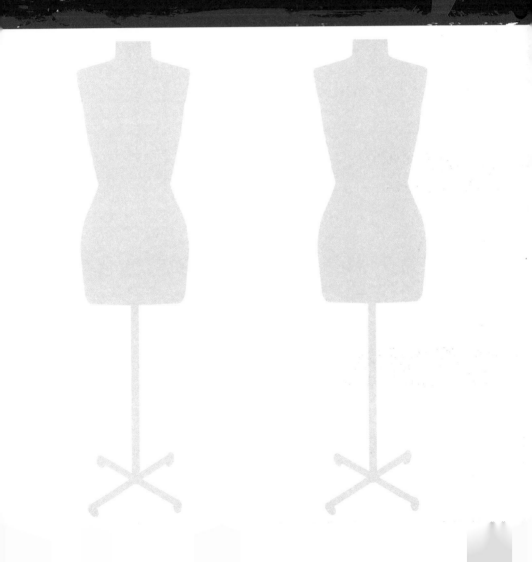

# Stow Away!

Every girl relies on her purse, clutch, and backpack to store her most important items! Below, fill in some info on these lifesavers.

## Purse:

What color is it? _____

Material? _____

What's in it right now? _____
_____

## Clutch:

What color is it? _____

Material? _____

What's in it right now? _____
_____

## Backpack:

What color is it? _____

Material? _____

What's in it right now? _____
_____

# Nail Heaven!

These nails could use a SPLASH of color! Decorate them with polka dots, animal prints, or even some super fab nail polish.

# Shoe Hall of Fame

Shoes don't get enough credit—they do a lot of work! Here's a place to give ur shoes the recognition they deserve. Paste pictures or draw in the winners in each category below.

**FANTASTIC FLIP-FLOP**

**HOTTEST HEEL**

**SELF-ESTEEM-BOOSTER BOOTS**

**#1 SNEAKER**

**BEST BALLET FLAT**

# What Ur Everyday 'Do Says About U!

**I usually wear my hair . . .**

- A. in a ponytail.
- B. down.
- C. gathered in a messy bun.

**How often do u use hair products?**

- A. every day
- B. once a week
- C. only on special occasions

**If I wear a ponytail it's . . .**

- A. tight without any bumps.
- B. a side pony.
- C. loose at my neck.

**When I wear a headband it's . . .**

- A. sparkly.
- B. single colored.
- C. I never wear a headband unless I need my hair out of my face.

# Results

## Mostly A's:
### Clean-cut.

Ur hair is a reflection of u and u want to keep it looking great.

## Mostly B's:
### Go with the flow.

Ur hair may or may not cooperate, but u work with what you've got!

## Mostly C's:
### Neither here nor hair.

U like to keep things simple. If ur hair isn't working, you'll throw it up out of ur face.

# Fashion Fails

Whether it's plaid mixed with stripes or a tacky holiday sweater, everyone has fashion disasters! Write ur biggest fashion fails here.

# Blogosphere, Here I Come!

Fav fashion blog to visit? _____

Topic? _____ Number of visits per week? _____

What would UR fashion blog be like? Fill in the info below.

Blogger Name _____

Blog _____ Topic _____

Write ur first blog post here:

FAV OUTFIT

_____
_____
_____
_____
_____
_____
_____

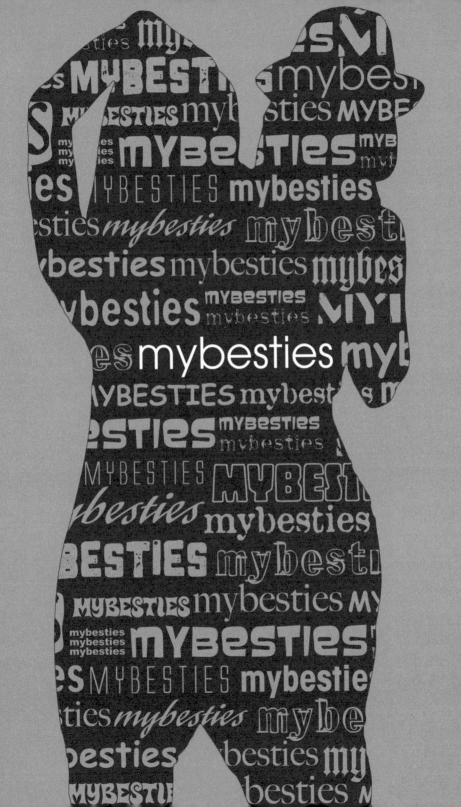

# BEST FRIENDS ARE ALWAYS THERE FOR U NO MATTER WHAT. BELOW, FILL IN UR BEST FRIENDS' NAMES AND ALL THE IMPORTANT INFO ABOUT THEM.

## BFF #1:

## BFF #2:

## BFF #3

**How long have u been friends?**

**How did u meet?**

**What are ur nicknames for each other?**

**What do u like most about this BFF?**

**How long have u been friends?**

**How did u meet?**

**What are ur nicknames for each other?**

**What do u like most about this BFF?**

**How long have u been friends?**

**How did u meet?**

**What are ur nicknames for each other?**

**What do u like most about this BFF?**

PASTE UR BFFS' PICS BELOW!

# How Well Do U Know Ur

$\mathscr{S}$it down with ur best friend. Use the questions below to find out how much she knows about u!

I ♥? _____

COLOR? _____

ANIMAL? _____

CRUSH? _____

WORD? _____

RESTAURANT? _____

CANDY? _____

SONG? _____

SNACK? _____

BAND? _____

ACTRESS? _____

ACTOR? _____

SINGER? _____

PIECE OF
CLOTHING? _____

Now flip the page and pass this book to ur friend.
Have her quiz u to see how much u really know about her!

# How Well Do U Know Ur

**Friend Edition!**

🎵 Sit down with ur best friend. Use the questions below to find out how much she knows about u!

I ♥? _____

COLOR? _____

ANIMAL? _____

CRUSH? _____

WORD? _____

RESTAURANT? _____

CANDY? _____

SONG? _____

SNACK? _____

BAND? _____

ACTRESS? _____

ACTOR? _____

SINGER? _____

PIECE OF CLOTHING? _____

# BFF BRACELETS

It doesn't matter if a friendship bracelet is a detailed design or a basic braid, these bracelets all have the same meaning— friendship is forever! Use the outlines to design ur BFF bracelets.

# TOP 5 BFF MOMENTS

All BFFs have those moments that define their friendship. Record the Top 5 here:

**1.**

**2.**

**3.**

**4.**

**5.**

# What Kind of Friend R U?

When my friends need me . . .

- A. I'm there for them in a flash.
- B. I'm there for them if I'm around.
- C. I tell them to come over for a girls' movie night.

My friends would describe me as . . .

- A. quiet and wise.
- B. mellow and kind.
- C. loud and hilarious.

My friends would say I'm best at . . .

- A. keeping a secret.
- B. giving advice.
- C. making plans.

When my friends do something that upsets me, I . . .

- A. keep it hush. No need to rock the boat!
- B. wait for the right time to tell them.
- C. tell them right away.

On a friend's birthday, I . . .

- A. make a card and a collage.
- B. buy a card and get everyone to sign it.
- C. throw a party!

49

# RESULTS

**MOSTLY  A's:**

*U r a Trustworthy & Comforting Friend!*

**MOSTLY B's:**

*U r a Sweet & Thoughtful Friend!*

**MOSTLY  C's:**

*U r a Fun & Outgoing Friend!*

# Friend Fails

Whether one of ur friends accidentally belched in front of her crush or wore the same dress as someone else to a dance, all of ur friends have had embarrassing moments! Write ur friends' biggest fail moments here.

# inside Joke

**Write down any words or phrases that only ur BESTIE would find funny.**

# WOULD U

# RATHER . . .

(circle answer)

Eat expired meat or smell a nasty armpit?

Not be able to talk for day or only be able to yell for a day?

Have the power to fly or be invisible?

Clean a random toilet once or not have to clean ur room for a month?

Be able to talk to animals or be able to read people's minds?

Go on an unlimited shopping spree or go on a trip to anywhere u wanted?

Be able to walk on the moon or breathe underwater?

# WOULD U RATHER...

(circle answer)

Eat expired meat or smell a nasty armpit?

Not be able to talk for day or only be able to yell for a day?

Have the power to fly or be invisible?

Clean a random toilet once or not have to clean ur room for a month?

Be able to talk to animals or be able to read people's minds?

Go on an unlimited shopping spree or go on a trip to anywhere u wanted?

Be able to walk on the moon or breathe underwater?

# Do U
# STALK ur FRIENDS
## Online?

EVERYONE IS ONLINE 24/7, BUT DO U TAKE IT TO
THE NEXT LEVEL? TAKE THIS QUIZ TO FIND OUT IF
U R A TOTAL STALKER!

**How often do u check ur friends' pages?**

 A. I get updates sent to my phone.

B. Whenever I remember to look.

**How often do u comment on ur friends' status updates?**

A. As soon as they post them.

B. When I feel like visiting their pages.

**Do u ever look at people's profiles who you've never met that ur friend is friends with?**

A. All the time!

B. Of course not!

**When ur friend posts a new album, u:**

A. Look through all their pictures . . . ALL of them!

B. Look at only a few pictures.

# RESULTS

## MOSTLY A's

### U r 100% stalker!

Every chance u get, u r
checking ur friends
out online.

## MOSTLY B's

### Mild case of stalkeritis.

U have stalking potential,
but u manage to keep
it under control.

# TRUTHS

# DARES

## TRUTHS

What's ur
favorite animated movie?

If u could have one
superpower, what would it be?

What's ur secret talent?

Who was ur first crush?

Who is ur crush now?

Have u ever declined
a friend request?

If u could be born as
any famous person in all of
history, who would it be?

Describe a dream
u once had.

If u and someone else were
the only people alive on Earth,
who would u want
the other person to be?

## DARES

Text ur crush!

Sing something for
thirty seconds.

Go into the kitchen and
eat a condiment.

Make an article of
clothing out of toilet
paper. Wear it.

Act out ur favorite
commercial.

Act out ur favorite
scene from a movie—
playing all the parts!

Talk without stopping
for one minute.

Impersonate a celeb
and let me guess
who it is.

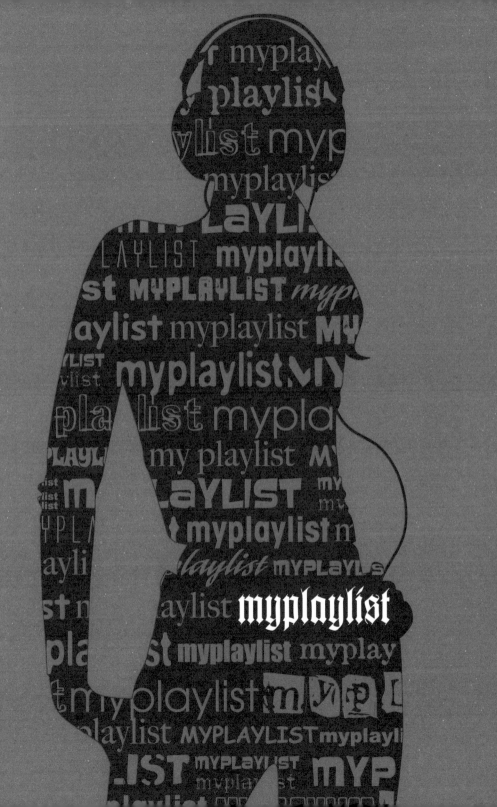

# I Can't Hear U!

(circle answer)

1. I ALWAYS LIKE BOY SINGERS   more / less   THAN GIRL SINGERS.

2. I PREFER MUSIC   with / without   LYRICS.

3. I LISTEN TO MY MUSIC WITH   big headphones. / tiny buds.

4. I WATCH ALL MY FAVORITE BANDS PERFORM   online. / in person.

5. I THINK THAT LIVE PERFORMANCES ARE   better / worse   THAN THE STUDIO VERSION.

6. WHEN IT COMES TO DOWNLOADS, I GO FOR THE   single song. / whole album.

7. WHEN I BLAST MY TUNES, I PUT THE SONGS ON   shuffle. / repeat.

# Ultimate Playlist?

1   Favorite song of all time:

2   Song that's stuck in my head:

3   Best dance song:

4   Best song to dance to (in ur room):

5   Best slow song:

6   Best song to wake up to:

7   Best song to fall asleep to:

8   Best song to work out to:

9   Best song to get ready to:

10  Best song to listen to when I'm sad:

11  Best song to listen to when I'm happy:

12  Best song to mellow out to:

13  Best broken-heart song:

14  Best song to sing along with:

15  My theme song:

**ROCK STARS ARE KNOWN FOR ROCKING LOTS OF TATTOOS. ADD ON TO THIS MUSICIAN'S ARM WITH ALL SORTS OF TATS—**

**"I ♥ MOM," HEARTS, SKULLS, OR EVEN FAVORITE LYRICS!**

Music for Life

# Meaningful Song Lyrics

*Write them on the page below.*

WHO'S IN UR DREAM BAND?

BAND NAME

Choose celebrities and/or friends to join ur band. Cut out pictures of their faces and paste them in the grayed-out spaces.

NOW ROCK THE HOUSE!

# SONG TITLE SWITCH UP!

First, read the beginnings of each popular song title. Then, write down the first word that pops into ur head! The hottest pop stars made these songs into hits. Here's ur chance to make them unique!

TEENAGE _____

MOVES LIKE _____

WE FOUND _____

YOU AND _____

I WANNA _____

DON'T STOP THE _____

LOVE YOU LIKE A _____

TODAY WAS A _____

YOU BELONG WITH _____

I GOTTA _____

ROLLING IN THE _____

# What Type of MUSICIAN R U?

**U sing...**
- A. love ballads.
- B. rock songs.
- C. show tunes.

**On stage, u rock a...**
- A. flowy dress.
- B. leather jacket.
- C. sparkly gown.

**When u r not performing, u r...**
- A. at home, writing poetry.
- B. at a club listening to a hot new band.
- C. attending a Broadway musical.

MYBOOK STAGE MIX

# RESULTS

## MOSTLY A's

U r a strong singer with a romantic side.

## MOSTLY B's

U r a rocker ready to bring down the house!

## MOSTLY C's

U r a total diva. No one is going to steal ur spotlight!

# TOPPING THE CHARTS

*Track 1*:                          *Track 4*:

*Track 2*:                          *Track 5*:

*Track 3*:                          *Track 6*:

# SURF OR TURF?

Some musicians are also surfers or skateboarders. Which would u rock?
Make over this surfboard and skateboard to reflect ur on-the-move style!

# Dancing
## to Ur Own
# Tune

### WHAT SONGS PLAY IN UR HEAD (OR IN UR EARS!) AS U GO ABOUT UR DAY?

WAKING UP IN THE A.M.:

EATING BREAKFAST:

TRAVELING TO SCHOOL:

GOSSIPING IN HOMEROOM:

WAITING FOR CLASS TO START:

MUNCHING ON LUNCH:

DAYDREAMING IN CLASS:

DOING HOMEWORK:

EATING DINNER:

TURNING OUT THE LIGHTS:

# WHAT'S UR MUSIC MENTALITY?

Put on ur fav song and find out what ur music habits say about u:    (circle answer)

The worst feeling is when I love a band that no one knows and then everyone knows them.

**YES or NO**

I listen to my favorite song on repeat.

**YES or NO**

I sing out loud in the car even if I don't know the words.

**YES or NO**

If I don't like a song, I skip past it immediately.

**YES or NO**

Mostly Yes's: U r a Music Maniac!
Mostly No's: U r a Music Maniac-In-Training!

TICKET
$83.00
10/25
8:00pm
FLOOR
BAD FLOOR
2
56
31408453

PRESENTING
THE AMAZING SEVEN
METROPOLITAN GARDEN
NEW YORK CITY, NY
FRI OCT 25, 8:00 PM

31497713B852

# Song Fails

Whether it's super-corny lyrics or the same beats over and over again, some songs are EPIC fails! Write ur fav song fails here.

# Unleash the Songwriter Inside U!

Have u ever wanted to have ur very own song? Well, now's ur chance! Use the word bank below to get started and let the creativity flow from ur mind to ur pen and onto the page!

| | | | |
|---|---|---|---|
| LOVE | FOREVER | YOU | FALL |
| BRAVE | HOLD | CATCH | LOOK |
| BEAUTY | STRONG | HEARTBEAT | STAR |
| CRASH | I COULD | MAKE WAVES | RUN |

# DECORATE UR LOCKER!

Most days ur locker looks pretty lame... unless ur friend decorates it 4 u on ur b-day!

GIVE UR LOCKER A MAKEOVER! DESIGN UR IDEAL LOCKER HERE>>>

# WOULD U

# RATHER...

(circle answer)

Have extra homework or a pop quiz?

Run the school-spirit committee or a bake sale?

Have someone keep kicking ur seat or spill a drink on ur keyboard?

Watch a video in class or an assembly in the auditorium?

## AND WHEN IT COMES TO UR SCHOOL CRUSH, WOULD U RATHER...

Be lab partners or be in a group presentation together?

Ask him to be a study buddy or to remind u when hw is due?

Sit next to each other on the bus or at an assembly?

Play on his team in gym class or against him in volleyball?

# Teacher Hall of Fame

**W**hich teachers will make it into ur Hall of Fame? Assign ur teachers each of these awesome awards!

COOLEST EVER

MOST LIKELY TO HELP U OUTSIDE OF CLASS

BEST JOKESTER

EINSTEIN

WILL BE REMEMBERED FOREVER

# SAY "CHEESE"!

**P**aste ur best and worst EVER school photos below. Feel free to add mustaches, eyeglasses, or other doodles—just like u would in ur yearbook!

# TOP 5 SCHOOL SUPPLIES

Which school supplies could u simply not live without?
List them below.

**1.**
### WHAT IS IT?
_____
WHY IS IT A MUST-HAVE ITEM?

**2.**
### WHAT IS IT?
_____
WHY IS IT A MUST-HAVE ITEM?

**3.**
### WHAT IS IT?
_____
WHY IS IT A MUST-HAVE ITEM?

**4.**
### WHAT IS IT?
_____
WHY IS IT A MUST-HAVE ITEM?

**5.**
### WHAT IS IT?
_____
WHY IS IT A MUST-HAVE ITEM?

# R U a Procrastinator?

EVERYONE PUTS OFF SCHOOLWORK FROM TIME TO TIME, BUT SOME PEOPLE ARE SERIOUS PROCRASTINATORS. TAKE THE QUIZ BELOW TO FIND OUT IF U R ONE OF THEM!

**When u get home from school u . . .**

A. set down ur bag and get right to work!

B. make yourself a snack and then look over ur homework.

C. go online until dinnertime.

**The day before an essay is due u . . .**

A. relax! Ur essay has been finished for days.

B. give it a read-through to fix any last-minute errors.

C. stay up late to get it done.

**The main reason u would wait to do homework is:**

A. U have so many projects on ur plate.

B. There's a good show on TV.

C. U work best under pressure!

**When u forget ur homework, u . . .**

A. Forget my homework?! Never!

B. apologize and make up the work ASAP.

C. claim ur dog ate it.

**In homeroom, u . . .**

A. talk with ur friends.

B. double-check ur homework.

C. do ur homework.

*Deadline!*

83

# RESULTS

## MOSTLY A's:

### *On Time Every Time.*

Procrastinating is not an option. U like getting ur work done right away!

## MOSTLY B's:

### *Mild Procrastinator.*

Sometimes u put off work to call a friend, but most of the time u r on top of ur projects.

## MOSTLY C's:

### *Total Procrastinator.*

U always put things off until the very last minute. Ur fav phrase is: "I'll get to it later."

# XTRA CURRICULAR ACTIVITIES

## Which would u pick?

(circle answer)

Debate Club or Chess Club

Study Group or Student Government

Theater or Soccer

Choir or Band

School Newspaper Reporter
or
Literary Mag Contributor

## START UR VERY OWN CLUB!

Use the space below to write ur club mission, which teacher would sponsor it, and how u would get ur classmates to join. Then go out and make it happen!

# CLASS YEARBOOK

Paste pictures below to nominate your friends for these funny yearbook awards!

## CLASS CLOWN

NAME:

## BEST DRESSED

NAME:

## BRAINIAC

NAME:

## ATHLETE

NAME:

## DRAMA QUEEN

NAME:

## BASKET CASE

NAME:

## LITTLE MISS SUNSHINE

NAME:

## CRIMINAL

NAME:

## PRINCESS

NAME:

**School Edition!**

**a** Ask ur crush to the school dance?_____

**B** Best thing about school?_____

**C** Class u love the most?_____

**d** Dot ur i's with hearts?_____

**e** Extracurricular of choice?_____

**f** First to raise ur hand?_____

**g** Grades are_____.

**h** Hardest class?_____

**i** In class, I am most likely to_____.

**J** Jump 4 joy when u get a good grade?_____

**k** Key to getting good grades?_____

**L** Like most of ur teachers?_____

Making new friends is_____.

Never played hooky?_____

Occasionally fall asleep in class?_____

Projects r best done solo or in a group?_____

Quit something or stick it through?_____

Run track? Run anything?_____

Sign up 4 events?_____

Test-taking makes me_____.

U sit in the front row?_____

Valentine's Day cards 4 all ur friends?_____

Weirdest teacher EVER?_____

Xtra Credit?_____

Yawn during which class?_____

Zoom straight home after the bell rings?_____

m n o p q r s t u v w x y z

# ANATOMY OF A SCHOOL LUNCH

Some school lunches make the grade while others are barely edible. Draw the grossest school lunch EVER!

# FriEND

## Collage

Print out pics of u and ur close school friends from each of ur online pages.

Make a collage here! Add ridiculous captions.

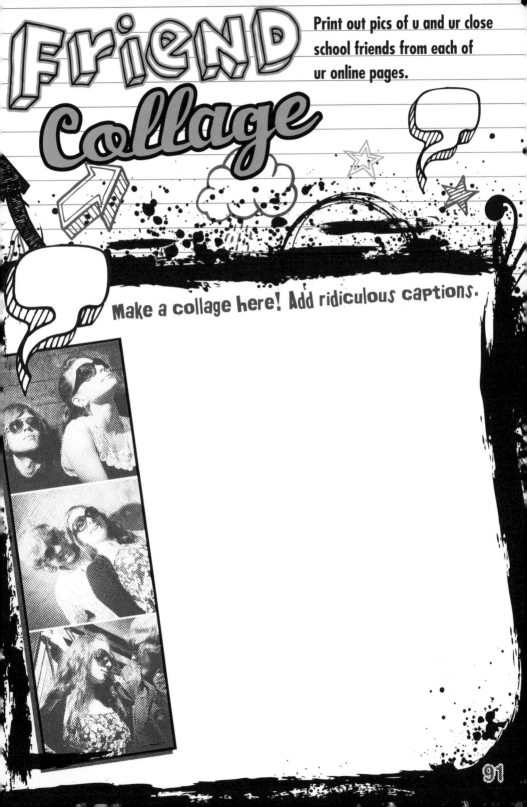

# School Fails

Whether u studied the wrong subject for ur midterm or forgot ur locker combo, everyone has had fails at school! Write ur biggest school fails here.

Write

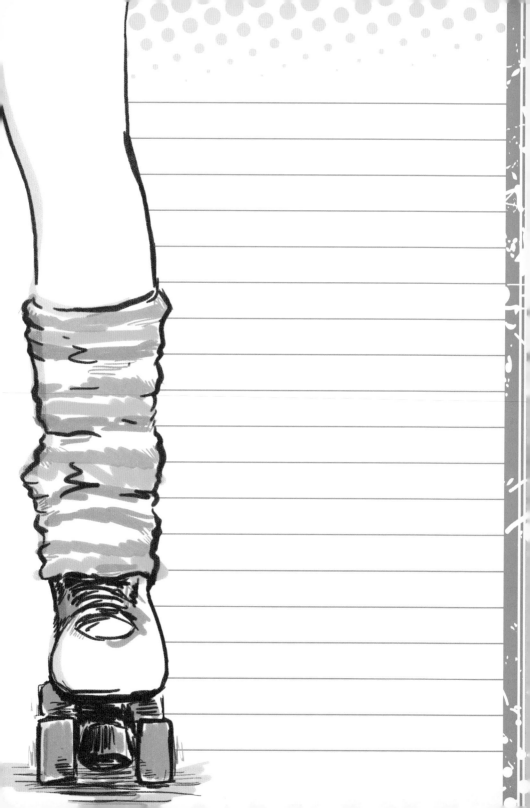

# WOULD U

# RATHER. . .

Become the president or a rock star?

Be a talented singer or writer?

Live in a warm or cool climate?

Run ur own restaurant or be a food critic?

Have a small city apartment or a big house in the 'burbs?

Have a backyard with a tire swing or a pool with a diving board?

Live closer to ur family or to the beach?

Travel to every continent or to Mars?

# SHAKE THINGS UP!

1. _____
2. _____
3. _____
4. _____
5. _____
6. _____
7. _____
8. _____
9. _____
10. _____

Write 10 yes-or-no questions about ur future—hopes, boys, wishes, dreams. Then shake the book and turn the page to find out which ones will come true!

AND MY BOOK SAYS . . .

1. Most likely!

2. Ask again later . . .

3. All signs point to yes!

4. No.

5. Very doubtful.

6. Without a doubt!

7. Outlook is good for this one!

8. Cannot predict now . . .

9. Yes!

10. U can count on it!

# FiLL in this Entire paGE using only ur FAV COLOR. Add things u hope to hAVE in ur Future!

USE ANYTHING— CRAYONS, PENCILS, PiCTURES, CLOTH—AS LONG AS IT'S UR FAV COLOR.

**H**ave ur bestie draw ticks in the box on this page until u say stop. Then, beginning with *MANSION*, have her count through ur answer choices for each item below in order. When she reaches ur number of ticks, she should cross off that item. Then, she should start over at the next answer after the one she just crossed off, and repeat until there is only one item left in each category. When she's done, you'll have all the deets for future u!

# Ultimate ~~|||| ||~~
# MASH

*mansion  apartment  shack  house*

TICKS

START HERE: *1.* MANSION    *2.* APARTMENT    *3.* SHACK    *4.* HOUSE

**BESTIE IN CHARGE: FILL IN THESE BLANKS!**

## Boys
5. _____
6. _____
7. _____
8. _____

## Job
9. TEACHER
10. LAWYER
11. VET
12. BEEKEEPER

## Place
13. LOS ANGELES
14. DALLAS
15. NEW YORK
16. ANTARCTICA

## Car
17. CONVERTIBLE
18. SUV
19. HYBRID
20. MINIVAN

## Pet
21. DOG
22. CAT
23. FISH
24. SKUNK

# Now help ur bestie predict her future!

## Ultimate ~~IIII II~~ MASH

mansion    apartment    shack    house

**Friend Edition!**

TICKS

START HERE: **1. MANSION**    **2. APARTMENT**    **3. SHACK**    **4. HOUSE**

FILL IN THESE BLANKS FOR UR BESTIE!

### Boys
5. _____
6. _____
7. _____
8. _____

### Job
9. TEACHER
10. LAWYER
11. VET
12. BEEKEEPER

### Place
13. LOS ANGELES
14. DALLAS
15. NEW YORK
16. ANTARCTICA

### Car
17. CONVERTIBLE
18. SUV
19. HYBRID
20. MINIVAN

### Pet
21. DOG
22. CAT
23. FISH
24. SKUNK

# WHAT WILL BE, WILL BE...

Break out ur crystal ball to see where you'll be in 20 years! Write the 1st sentence to a story about ur future. Pass the book to ur friend and have her write the next sentence. Keep switching off until u have a finished story!

# Future Career?

Ur fav class in school is . . .

- A. drama.
- B. math
- C. English.
- D. gym.

When u need to solve a problem u . . .

- A. talk about the problem with family and friends.
- B. run the numbers!
- C. write out a pros-and-cons list.
- D. run and run and run until u decide.

If u have to give a presentation u . . .

- A. perform a skit to get ur point across.
- B. support ur presentation with charts and graphs.
- C. write an essay and read it aloud to the class.
- D. use a sports analogy to illustrate ur point.

Ur fav after-school activity is . . .

- A. drama club.
- B. mathletes meeting.
- C. poetry workshop.
- D. sports practice.

**103**

# RESULTS

## MOSTLY A's:

### Artist Extraordinaire!

U have a strong artistic side — u love performing and speaking in front of a crowd.

**Ideal jobs:** artist, actor, designer, film/theater critic, lawyer.

## MOSTLY B's:

### Math Whiz!

U have a passion for crunching numbers.

**Ideal jobs:** accountant, scientist, statistician, stockbroker, doctor.

## MOSTLY C's:

### Wordsmith!

Writing is ur strength; when u can express yourself on paper, u will.

**Ideal jobs:** writer, editor, journalist, poet, English professor.

## MOSTLY D's:

### #1 Athlete!

Sports are in ur blood, so u won't want to sit behind a desk all day.

**Ideal jobs:** physical therapist, sports trainer, professional athlete, sports agent, team coach.

# To-Be-Tweeted

What will u be tweeting in the future? Write some predictions below—with only 140 characters per entry. (That means a TOTAL of only 140 letters, numbers, and punctuation marks!) Can u limit yourself?

**Tweet:**      **Date:** _____

_____
_____
_____
_____

**Tweet:**      **Date:** _____

_____
_____
_____
_____

**Tweet:**      **Date:** _____

_____
_____
_____
_____

# Future Fails

Whether u spill something on ur prom dress or ur college roommate is a Martian, there's no escaping ur future fails! Write what u think ur future fails will be here.

# TIME CAPSULE

1) Use the next page to write a letter to ur future self. Don't forget to let her know what life is like in the present! Then, tear out this page.

2) Next, collect the following items:
   - an empty shoe box
   - a picture of yourself
   - a magazine
   - movie-ticket stubs
   - a picture of ur favorite food
   - anything else u want to include!

3) Gather these items (including ur letter) and place them in ur time capsule (the shoe box!). Hide the box in the farthest corner of ur closet, or place it in a plastic bag and then bury it out in the yard!

4) Mark ur calendar YEARS from now to remind yourself to uncover ur time capsule. Prepare for ur blast from the past!

DATE _____

# DEAR FUTURE ME, _____

_____

_____

_____

_____

_____

_____

_____

_____

_____

_____

_____

_____

_____

_____

_____

_____

_____

_____

_____

# Circle one word in each numbered box.

**1.**
CHEERFUL
GIGGLY
SMELLY
GOOEY

**2.**
SHOWER CURTAINS
JAM JARS
CARDBOARD BOXES
FISH TANKS

**3.**
WASHES
SEWS
BAKES
SINGS

**4.**
HIGH HEELS
THROW PILLOWS
MISMATCHED SOCKS
PURPLE PENS

**5.**
IGUANA
FACE
TOILET
HAIRDRYER

**6.**
ZIT
MUSTACHE
FOOT
JELLYFISH

**7.**
RED VELVET CUPCAKE
FLYING MONKEY
MAGIC CARPET
HOT-AIR BALLOON

**8.**
BLUEBERRY PIE
GIANT SQUID
TACKY HOLIDAY SWEATER
HUGE CHOCOLATE CHIP

**9.**
UGLY WIG
MOLDY CHEESE
STUFFED ANIMAL
INCHWORM

**10.**
LIMA BEAN
POODLE
COWBOY
HAM SANDWICH

# Say WHAT?!

Now fill in the numbered blanks in these sentences. Read ur wacky futuristic story aloud to a friend!

A _____ (7.) has been spotted in the northern sky! You are preparing for a/an _____ (9.) invasion by stocking your shelves with _____ (4.). The Martians are going to be very _____ (1.) when they first arrive. Welcome them with open _____ (2.) and a/an _____ (6.) on your face. The future is here, so make friends with your nearest _____ (10.) before a _____ (8.) lands on your _____ (5.) and _____ (3.) you to outer space!

109

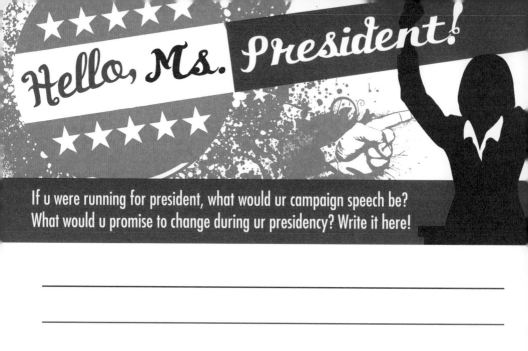

# Hello, Ms. President!

If u were running for president, what would ur campaign speech be? What would u promise to change during ur presidency? Write it here!

_____

_____

_____

_____

_____

_____

_____

_____

_____

_____

_____

_____

_____

_____

_____

# Make A Statement!

## FILL IN THE BLANKS:

BE A DREAMER AND A

NEVER LEAVE THE HOUSE WITHOUT

STRIPED SOCKS ARE SOOOOOO

NEON PINK IS

ALWAYS BE HONEST WITH

BLUEBERRY PANCAKES TASTE

ALWAYS LOOK

FLYING UNICORNS ARE

PLAID SKIRTS ARE THE

DON'T LOOK

SLEEP IS

TEDDY BEARS ARE SOOOOOO

ALWAYS WEAR

BELIEVE IN

**CARPÉ DiEM!**

car·pé di·em · (car-pay dee-em) Latin. Seize the day; enjoy the present, as opposed to placing all hope in the future.